Walking in the Light

Affirming the Presence Hour by Hour

David Adam

kevin mayhew

First published in 2005 by

KEVIN MAYHEW LTD
Buxhall, Stowmarket, Suffolk, IP14 3BW
E-mail: info@kevinmayhewltd.com

9 8 7 6 5 4 3 2 1 0

ISBN 184417 356 9
Catalogue No 1500774

Cover design by Angela Selfe
Edited by Marian Reid
Typesetting by Richard Weaver

Printed and bound in Great Britain

Contents

David Adam was the Vicar of Lindisfarne, off the Northumbrian coast, for thirteen years until he retired in March 2003. His work involved ministering to thousands of pilgrims and other visitors. He is the author of many inspiring books on spirituality and prayer, and his Celtic writings have rekindled a keen interest in our Christian heritage.

Introduction

The prayers in this book are arranged around the idea of the twelve hours of the day. The scriptural basis for this are the words of Jesus in John 11:9, 'Are there not twelve hours in the day? If anyone walks in the day, he does not stumble, because he sees the light of this world.' Here is an opportunity to walk in the light not only of the world but of the Lord. Come, accept this invitation and walk in the light of the Lord. The twelve chapters, one for each hour, represent twelve different aspects of daily discipleship under the following headings:

1. Waking
2. On the Road
3. The Daily Round
4. Watching for Christ and His Kingdom
5. In the Desert
6. Darkness at Midday
7. Confession and Forgiveness
8. Growing in Grace
9. Peace in God's Presence
10. Thanks and Praise
11. At the End of the Day
12. All Through the Night

You may find you do not use all the hours but keep returning to one particular hour, and this is fine. Some hours of the day are always more special to us than others. We are not so concerned to get through chronological time as to enjoy knowing that our times are fulfilled. It is more important to have vital relationships and be in touch with all that is around us than to say: 'That's another day done.' Use this book to invent your own hours with your own prayers and your own hymn choices. Strangely, sometimes when it is hard to say prayers I find I can quietly hum them! Know that, whatever the time, God is with you and he waits for you to turn to him.

Let me tell you of a little of my own experience of growing in prayer and the awareness of the presence. At the age of eighteen I entered the Kelham Theological College, run by the Society of the Sacred Mission. I learnt to live alongside their rule of life and that meant going to church to pray many times a day. Monastic communities were used to going to church seven times a day. In fact, if I include my twenty minutes for meditation, I was only going six times a day. Time in church was to be balanced with time for study and time for manual work. Some days it would seem that prayers interfered with our work: at other times our work seemed to disrupt our prayer. On the best days we knew that our work, our prayers, our study and our rest all enriched each other: they were not separate from each other but interwoven like a beautiful tapestry. To lose one of the strands would have broken the harmony of the whole. I gradually learnt that a day without prayer was a day when I was impoverished. Prayer enriches my life day by day and my daily living should enrich my prayers. I was learning to walk in the light of the Lord.

I was beginning to learn to live the way of the psalmist when he said: 'Seven times a day I praise thee' (Psalm 119:164). The early monks learnt all the psalms off by heart (and I mean heart, not head, for they learnt them in worship). As there were no written books for individuals, they had to memorise the psalms to take part in worship. Most monastic communities said Psalm 119 (all 176 verses) every day, so it was one of the first psalms to be learnt. In my first year at Kelham all the psalms were placed in my heart.

The first book I tried to use for meditation was *The Practice of the Presence of God* by Brother Lawrence. This encouraged me to turn to God when I was shovelling coal, writing an essay, or doing gardening. I was beginning to learn to turn to God quite naturally throughout the hours of the day. There was no need to stop what I was doing. I could talk to him as easily as to any other person present. Sometimes it was of great importance to stop everything and turn to him with undivided attention. Most waking hours included a little turning to God. Yet, when I came across St Patrick's statement about his prayers, it still came as a shock. He said: 'I prayed a hundred prayers in the daytime and almost as many at night.' Here was someone with a living and loving relationship with God. I still had a long way to go! Yet in a sense I did not, for God was always there.

In his first letter to the Thessalonians, St Paul writes: 'Pray without ceasing' (1 Thessalonians 5:17). I understood this to be an awareness of a permanent and abiding relationship with God. But you cannot have a relationship with someone if you do not speak to that person regularly. Throughout the day it is good to take little moments out and speak to the ever-present God. It is hoped that the layers of this little book will set you on a course that you will follow for the rest of your life. Let the presence of God enrich each hour and let your experiences in life deepen your awareness of the love and forgiveness of God. The words of a hymn express what most of the book is about for it is about our need and our desire for God:

I need thee every hour,
most gracious Lord;
no tender voice like thine
can peace afford.

Chorus

I need thee, O I need thee,
every hour I need thee;
O bless me now, my Saviour,
I come to thee.

I need thee every hour,
stay thou near by;
temptations lose their power
when thou art nigh.

I need thee every hour,
in joy or pain;
come quickly abide
or life is in vain.

I need thee every hour,
teach me thy will;
and rich promises
in me fulfil.

Annie Sherwood Hawks (1835-1918)

1
WAKING

New every morning is the love
our wakening and uprising prove;
through sleep and darkness safely brought,
restored to life, and power, and thought.

John Keble (1792-1866)

Lord, open my eyes to your presence:
open my ears to your call.
Open my lips to sing your praises.
Open my heart to your great love.
May I awaken out of sleep
that I may be aware of you,
glimpse at your great glory
and enjoy your presence.
Let nothing take me from you
that I may know and love you.

Open my eyes this day to your presence
that I may know that I dwell in you
and be aware that you are in me.
Grant me a glimpse of your great glory,
as I desire you and seek your love.
As I seek, grant me to find,
as I find, grant me to be found by you;
through Christ our Lord who comes this day.

I start this day
in the presence of the Father,
in the peace of Christ the Saviour,
in the power of the Holy Spirit.
I start this day
in the love of the Holy Three,
in the might of the Trinity.

Christ, the light of the world, come to me
and fill my life with glory.
Give me the power to do your will
and serve you, whose service is perfect freedom.
And may the Blessing of God Almighty,
    the Father, the Son and the Holy Spirit,
be with me and my loved ones always.

Blessed are you, Lord God of our ancestors,
your light dispelled their darkness:
you revealed to them your presence and your love.
You spoke to them as you would to friends.
May I too be aware of your coming,
rejoice in your presence,
walk in your light,
and abide in your love today and all my days.

Blessed are you, Lord God of all creation,
you created light out of darkness
and brought us to the glorious light of day.

Through men and women of vision,
you reveal your light and your presence to us:
you offer to us the glorious freedom of the children of God.
I come to walk in your light and in your love.
Blessed are you, Father, Son and Holy Spirit.

Blessed are you, Lord God of all creation,
from the rising of the sun to its setting,
your glory is proclaimed in all the world.
Your presence has brought light to our darkness
and a new radiance to the world.
As you call me into your marvellous light,
may I offer my life and talents to you,
may my lips proclaim your praise,
and may I go on my way rejoicing.
Blessed be God for ever.

Lord, give me
a quiet heart, that I may hear you:
a generous heart, that I may receive you:
an obedient heart, that I may serve you:
a pure heart, that I may see you:
a loving heart, that I may abide in you
this day and for ever.

2
_____ ON THE ROAD _____

Alone with none but thee, my God
I journey on my way.
What need I fear when thou art near,
O King of night and day?
More safe I am within thy hand
than if a host did round me stand.

Columba (521-597)

Lord, on the way of goodness,
when I stumble lift me up,
when I stray guide me back to you,
when I get lost lead me back to your presence.
Bring me into the way that leads to eternal life,
that I may serve you in joy and love:
through Jesus Christ our Lord.

May the strength of God guide me.
May the power of God preserve me.
May the wisdom of God instruct me.
May the hand of God protect me.
May the way of God direct me.
May the host of God shield me against the snares of the evil
    one and the temptations of the world.
May Christ be with me, Christ before me, Christ behind me,
Christ beneath me, Christ above me.
May your salvation, O Lord, be mine this day and evermore.

O God,
who by the leading of a star brought the wise men
    to Bethlehem,
guide me through each day and night on my journey
    of faith.
Lord, give me the courage to persevere,
that I am not put off in my search for you.
May I witness to your gospel and rejoice in your glory.
May I seek to do your will until I enter the fullness of
    your kingdom.
I ask this in the name of Jesus who came and lived among us.

May the bright light of Christ enlighten my heart,
shine in my mind and direct my journeying,
and give light to the world.

May Christ the Light of the World,
scatter the darkness about me and before me.
May the bright light of Christ lead me
into the ways of peace and goodwill towards all.

May the Love of God go with me,
wherever he calls me.
May he guide me through the desert,
protect me through the storm.
May he give light in my darkness
and courage to my fearful heart;
and may the blessing of God Almighty, the Father,
    the Son and the Holy Spirit, remain with me always.

May the Love of God go with me,
wherever he calls me.
May he guide me through the desert,
protect me through the storm.
May he give light in my darkness
and courage to my fearful heart;
and may the blessing of God Almighty, the Father,
   the Son and the Holy Spirit, remain with me always.

3
_____THE DAILY ROUND_____

> The trivial round, the common task,
> will furnish all we ought to ask:
> room to deny ourselves, a road
> to bring us daily nearer God.
>
> John Keble (1792-1866)

Blessed are you, Lord God of all creation.
To you be praise and glory for ever!
In the darkness of this passing age your light has shone out.
You have not forced yourself upon us,
but you only come if we so will it.
As I rejoice in the obedience of the blessed Virgin,
may I accept you into my life and home,
knowing that you have come to dwell with me.
Blessed be God for ever.

Lord, grant that I may hear and receive your Holy Word,
not only with my ears, but with my heart and mind also,
that I may show forth its fruit in my life,
for the benefit of all and to the glory of your holy name.

Blessed are you, Lord God of all creation,
to you be praise and glory for ever!
Your messenger, John the Baptist,
was a shining and burning light in the darkness.

He spoke the words of a prophet
and proclaimed forgiveness and the kingdom.
He prepared the way for the coming of the Lord.
May I share in his witness to the light,
that true Light which has come into the world,
and rejoice that the Christ dispels my darkness.
Blessed are you, God, for ever.

Inspire me, O Lord, by the life and teaching of John
    the Baptist.
May I learn to live simply, that others may simply live:
let me turn to you each day and rise in your presence.
Let me seek forgiveness of all that is past and direction for
    the future,
that I may be a herald of Christ and prepare for his coming;
that I may live and work for his Kingdom, where you reign,
O Father, with the Son and the Holy Spirit;
    one God now and for ever.

Help me to be the person you want me to be,
and to achieve what you want me to do,
that I may go out in confidence
and serve you all my days:
Through Jesus Christ our Lord, who is alive and reigns
    with you and the Holy Spirit,
one God now and forever. Amen.

For all who share in your creative spirit,
for all who are co-creators,
for all who are parents, all who are caring for others,
for all who work the land, all who provide us with food,
Creator, hear my prayer.

For artists, musicians and craft workers,
for teachers, preachers, doctors and nurses,
for all who work in conservation,
for those who improve and enrich our environment,
Creator, hear my prayer.

For those who have lost their vocation,
for all who feel their talents are wasted,
for all who are restricted by poverty or oppression,
for all who go unnoticed or are unappreciated,
Creator, hear my prayer.

Father of all creation, I thank you that you have given us a
world rich in resources, and invited us to share in your
creative spirit. Help me to accept with joy the abilities
you have given me, neither wasting nor misusing your
creation. May I act with reverence and love towards all
things and so reflect the great love you have for your
creation.

May the Father guard me and each action,
the Son protect me and each thought,
the Spirit guide me in all my dealings,
and the blessing of the Giver of all good gifts
be upon me and all that I do, now and evermore.

4
WATCHING FOR CHRIST
——— AND HIS KINGDOM ———

Hark the glad sound! The Saviour comes,
the Saviour promised long;
let every heart prepare a throne,
and every voice a song.

Philip Doddridge (1702-51)

Lord, I look for you.
Open my eyes to your presence.
Maranatha! Come, Lord Jesus.

God of all love and beauty,
open my heart to welcome you,
that your Son Jesus Christ, in his coming,
may find me looking and longing for him
and may find in me a dwelling prepared for himself:
who is alive and reigns with you and the Holy Spirit,
One God now and for ever.

Come, Lord, be known to me.
As you came to earth, born of Mary,
come into my heart and home.

Come, Lord, be known to me.
As you became a little child,
help me to grow in awareness of you.

Come, Lord, be known to me.
As you walked this earth,
help me to walk and work with you.

Christ, risen in glory,
scatter the darkness
from my heart and mind
and from the world,
that I may live in the fullness of life
and in awareness of your glorious kingdom:
And the blessing of God Almighty, the Father,
the Son and the Holy Spirit, be upon me now and for ever.

Come, Lord God,
come to me.
Come as my king
and bring in your kingdom.

Rule in my heart,
God of love.
Come as my king
and bring in your kingdom.

Rule in my mind,
Prince of peace.
Come as my king
and bring in your kingdom.

Rule in all my doings,
Spirit of power.
Come as my king
and bring in your kingdom.

Come, Lord God,
come to me.
Come as my king
and bring in your kingdom.

Lord, you alone are my God.
your kingdom come in me as it is in heaven:
come in my heart as I desire to love you,
come in my mind as I seek to serve you,
come in my strength as I seek to obey you,
come to my eyes as I look for you,
come in my lips as I speak of you,
come to my hands as I work for you.
Lord, you alone are my God,
your kingdom come in me as it is in heaven.

5
IN THE DESERT

I hunger and I thirst;
Jesus, my manna be:
ye living waters, burst
out of the rock for me.

Rough paths my feet have trod
since first their course began;
feed me, thou Bread of God,
help me, thou Son of Man.

For still the desert lies
my thirsting soul before;
O living waters, rise
within me evermore.

John Samuel Bewley Monsell (1811-75)

God of the desert,
there you spoke to Moses,
there you prepared John the Baptist,
let me know that you are with me.
When my feelings do not sense you,
when my mind begins to doubt you,
continue as my guardian and guide.
Lead me out of my darkness into light,
until I come out of the wilderness
and share the joys of the Promised Land.

O God, I hunger and I thirst for you,
I seek and I search for you,
my life is not satisfied with material things alone.
Come fill my emptiness with your presence:
strengthen my weakness with your power:
still my restlessness with your abiding peace.
Let me rejoice in your presence,
    as in finding an oasis in the desert,
for I hunger and thirst for you, God of life and love.

Lord, I turn to you, the Bread of Life,
I do not have to seek your presence. You are ever with me.
I am daily in your presence and your love.
Lord, make me aware of you.
Fill me with your Spirit.
In my emptiness, my loneliness,
    my boredom, let me hear your call,
for there is a space for you and for you alone.
Lord, let me relax in your presence
until my life is filled with you and your peace.

O God of light and hope, I pray
for all who are in darkness and despair;
for those who doubt your presence and your love;
for all in the wilderness and who find it difficult to pray;
for those who have lost trust in themselves or faith in you.
God you are with each and everyone,
and continue to be their protector and strength.
I pray for the day when they will rejoice in your presence
and in your abiding love. Through Jesus Christ our Lord.

6
———— DARKNESS AT MIDDAY ————

I need thy presence every passing hour;
what but thy grace can foil the tempter's power?
Who like thyself my guide and stay can be?
Through cloud and sunshine, O abide with me.

Henry Francis Lyte (1793-1847)

Lord, be with me: and guide me
when I am tempted to live below par,
when I fail to live up to my ideals,
when I settle for lower standards.
Lord, be with me: and guide me.

When I am full of doubt and disbelief,
when I am not sure of myself,
when my confidence is low.
Lord, be with me: and guide me.

When I am concerned only with material things,
when I seek only excitement and wonder,
when I am in danger of putting God to the test.
Lord, be with me: and guide me.

Teach me to come to you in the silence,
to make room for you in my life,
to offer you my loving heart.
Lord, be with me: and guide me.

That I may know your presence,
that I may experience your power,
that I may accept your peace.
Lord, be with me: and guide me.

When the days are dark and cold,
the Lord comes as he did to his people of old.
When the way is unknown and my future uncertain,
the Lord comes as he did to his people of old.
When I am in captivity and long to be free,
the Lord comes as he did to his people of old.
When I am in the wilderness and hunger and thirst,
the Lord comes as he did to his people of old.

To those who are seekers and travelling in the darkness,
the Lord comes as he came to the wise men.
To those who are not sure of the way and get lost,
the Lord comes as he came to the wise men.
To those who keep looking and longing,
the Lord comes as he came to the wise men.
To those who are watching and waiting,
the Lord comes as he came to the wise men.

Lord God, my Father,
by the temptations of Jesus
deliver me from evil.
By the triumph of Jesus
bring me into his kingdom.
By the resurrection of Jesus
bring me to the fullness of eternal life,
and the blessing of God Almighty, the Father, the Son and
    the Holy Spirit be upon me and remain with me always.

I go out in the love and power of God.
Lord, be with me and protect me in the darkness.
Lord, guide me into the way of peace.
Lord, strengthen me to do what you would have me do.
And the blessing of God Almighty, the Father,
    the Son and the Holy Spirit be upon me and my loved
    ones now and forever.

May the love of the Father enfold me,
the love of the Saviour uphold me,
the love of the Spirit surround me.
May I find in God a sure foundation:
and may the blessing of the Almighty
be upon me now and for ever.

May I find in Christ crucified
a sure ground for my faith,
a firm support for my hopes,
the assurance that sin is forgiven,
and the promise that life is eternal.
and the blessing of the holy Three
be upon me and my home now and for ever.

I rest in his presence and am aware of his love.
May his presence be a light to my darkness.
A candle in the dark.

7
CONFESSION AND FORGIVENESS

Dear Lord and Father of mankind,
forgive our foolish ways;
reclothe us in our rightful mind,
in purer lives thy service find,
in deeper reverence praise,
in deeper reverence praise.

John Greenleaf Whittier (1807-1892)

Creator God, forgive my lack of vision.
I have failed to acknowledge the world belongs to you.
I have not cared enough about the wellbeing of the world.
I have often wasted my talents and time and brought little
    to full growth.
I have not had enough respect for my neighbours or myself.
I have used words and actions that are not worthy of a
    co-creator.
Lord, forgive me, heal me, redeem me and sustain me.

For my failure to listen, Lord forgive me.
For my hardness of heart, Lord forgive me.
For my insensitivity to others, Lord forgive me.
For my fixed attitudes, Lord forgive me.
For my overcrowded life, Lord forgive me.
For my overfilled days, Lord forgive me.
For my lack of concern, Lord forgive me.
For my unwillingness to change, Lord forgive me.
For my narrowness of vision, Lord forgive me.
For my turning away from you, Lord forgive me.

Almighty God, have mercy upon me, forgive me my sins,
   confirm and strengthen me in all goodness, and continue
   to give me a share in creation, through Jesus Christ my
   Saviour, who lives and reigns with you and the Holy
   Spirit now and forever.

When relationships are difficult and I need a loving presence,
the Lord comes as he did to his people of old.
When I fail in my faithfulness and need forgiveness,
the Lord comes as he did to his people of old.
When life is empty and chaos seems to have taken over,
the Lord comes as he did to his people of old.
When evil triumphs and I feel defeated,
the Lord comes as he did to his people of old.
When I am wrung out and am unable to rise,
the Lord comes as he did to his people of old.

When I struggle to be faithful and to say my prayers,
the Lord comes as he came to his people of old.
When I am willing to let go for the sake of God,
the Lord comes as he came to his people of old.
When I attempt to proclaim the gospel,
the Lord comes as he came to his people of old.
When I patiently await his coming,
the Lord comes as he came to his people of old.

He comes to me today as he came yesterday.
He will come again tomorrow, as he came today.
He comes to me always.
I welcome him and say, 'Come, Lord Jesus.'

God, in your love and forgiveness, accept me.
Christ, in your love and salvation, bring me home.
Holy Spirit, in your mighty power, restore and refresh me.
The grace of God, go with me now and always.

8
_____ GROWING IN GRACE _____

Amazing grace! How sweet the sound
that saved a wretch like me.
I once was lost, but now am found;
was blind but now I see.

'Twas grace that taught my heart to fear,
and grace my fears relieved.
How precious did that grace appear
the hour I first believed.

John Newton (1725-1807)

Lord, lead me today
to a greater awareness,
to a firmer grasp of reality,
to a wider vision,
to a deeper sensitivity
to a response to wonder
and to a constant love for you.

Lord of the harvest, I call upon you,
that I may bring forth the fruits of the Spirit.
Let my life produce a good crop of love, joy, peace,
    patience, gentleness,
goodness, humility and self-control,
that I may work for the wellbeing of all
and reveal your glory in my life.

O God,
you created us for love and by your love.
For your love in caring for us,
for your love in providing for us,
I give you thanks and praise.

For your love revealed in seeking us,
for your love revealed in meeting us,
for your love revealed in accepting us,
I give you thanks and praise.

For your love revealed in forgiveness,
for your love revealed in your saving power,
for your love revealed in the resurrection,
I give you thanks and praise.

9
___ PEACE IN GOD'S PRESENCE ___

Drop thy still dews of quietness,
till all our strivings cease;
take from our souls the strain and stress,
and let our ordered lives confess
the beauty of thy peace.

John Greenleaf Whittier (1807-1892)

I place myself:
in the presence of the Father, who created me *out* of love
and *for* his love;
in the presence of the Son, who redeemed me *by* his love
and *for* his love;
in the presence of the Spirit, who sustains me *by* his love
and *for* his love.

Lord in the stillness speak to me,
in the emptiness come to me and fill me.
To my troubles come with your peace,
to my weakness come with your strength,
in my doubts and my fears abide with me.
Still the storms within me and let me find rest in you.

Lord,
as I enter into the stillness, calm my heart and my mind.
Let all the storms within me cease,
    and enfold me in your peace.
I come in weakness to you for strength.
I come in my sinfulness for your forgiveness.
I come wearied by life for your refreshing grace.
I come out of our darkness to your love and light.
Lord, renew, refresh, restore me by your presence
    and your power.

Peace, Lord, be in my heart and mind.
Peace, Lord, in my actions and in my dealings.
Peace, Lord, in my home and in all relationships.
Peace, Lord, in each community and in the world.
Peace, Lord, the deep, deep peace of God be upon me.
Peace, Lord, be within me and with me always.

10
_____ THANKS AND PRAISE _____

Praise, my soul, the King of Heaven;
to his feet thy tribute bring;
ransomed, healed, restored, forgiven,
who like me his praise should sing?
Praise him! Praise him!
Praise him! Praise him!
Praise the everlasting King.

Henry Francis Lyte (1793-1847)

For the magnificence of the universe,
God of all, I praise you.
For the majesty of the earth,
God of all, I praise you.
For the talents you have given me,
God of all, I praise you.
For all that I have achieved,
God of all, I praise you.
For your power within all things,
God of all, I praise you.

For fellowship and friendship, I give you thanks and praise.
For talents and sharing, I give you thanks and praise.
For growth and learning, I give you thanks and praise.
For faith and hope, I give you thanks and praise.
For the firm foundation of Christ, I give you thanks
and praise.

For your forgiveness and acceptance, glory to you, O Lord.
For your love in our redemption, glory to you, O Lord.
For your death and resurrection, glory to you, O Lord.
For your gift of life eternal, glory to you, O Lord.
For your presence with me always, glory to you, O Lord.

That I may rejoice in the Lord always, I ask in prayer.
That I may know him and the power of his resurrection,
    I ask in prayer.
That I may have life and life abundant, I ask in prayer.
That I may share in the glorious liberty of the children
    of God, I ask in prayer.
That I may dwell in him and he in us, I ask in prayer.

For the God who seeks me when I hide,
I give thanks and praise.
For the God who finds me when I seek,
I give thanks and praise.
For Moses bowing before the mystery of God,
I give thanks and praise.
For the disciples awaking on the mountain,
I give thanks and praise.
For Isaiah's awareness that God is on his throne,
I give thanks and praise.
For the obedience and Christ-bearing of Mary,
I give thanks and praise.
For the sustaining and renewing of Elijah,
I give thanks and praise.
For the angel's song to the shepherds,
I give thanks and praise.
For Ezekiel and new life to dry bones,
I give thanks and praise.

For the journeying and offering of the wise men,
I give thanks and praise.
For the coming of God into the world,
I give thanks and praise.
For his presence with me now,
I give thanks and praise.

Blessed are you, Lord God of all creation,
you are our light and our salvation.
To you be all praise and glory for ever.
In the darkness of this passing age
you sent your Son to be our Saviour.
The word became flesh and now dwells among us.
He descended and became human
that we might ascend and share in the divine.
As I rejoice in your presence with me now,
let your love fill my heart and my days
and your praises be on my lips.
Blessed be God for ever.

May the Christ, risen in glory, be known to dwell with me,
may the peace and joy of the risen Lord be upon me,
and the blessing of the Almighty, Father,
    Son and Holy Spirit,
be with me, now and for ever. Amen.

11
___ AT THE END OF THE DAY ___

Grant us thy peace upon our homeward way;
with thee began, with thee shall end the day:
guard thou the lips from sin, the hearts from shame,
that in this house have called upon thy name.

Grant us thy peace, Lord, through the coming night;
turn thou for us its darkness into light;
from harm and danger keep thy children free,
for dark and light are both alike to thee.

John Ellerton (1826-93)

God, the Creator, surround me with your presence,
Christ, the Redeemer, cover me with your love.
The Holy Spirit, the Strengthener,
    be about me to protect me.
That I may be immersed in the power and peace of God,
that the Holy Three may abide in me and I in them.
And may the blessing of God Almighty, the Father, the Son
    and the Holy Spirit, be upon me and remain with me
    and my loved ones now and always.

Good and gracious God
grant me a glimpse of your glory.
May your angels defend me,
your presence go with me,
your light guide me,
your love surround me.

And the blessing of God Almighty, the Father,
   the Son and the Holy Spirit,
     be upon me and my loved ones now and always.

The goodness of the Father,
the grace of Christ the Son,
the guidance of the Holy Spirit,
the glory of the Three in One
be with me now and always.

May the Lord in his coming
find me looking, longing and loving.

God, in your holiness, protect me,
Christ, in your majesty, save me,
Holy Spirit, on high, inspire me,
that my life may be full of peace and love.
And may the blessing of God Almighty, the Father,
the Son and the Holy Spirit be upon me now and evermore.

12
___ ALL THROUGH THE NIGHT ___

Grant us thy peace, Lord, through the coming night;
turn thou for us its darkness into light;
from harm and danger keep thy children free,
for dark and light are both alike to thee.

John Ellerton (1826-93)

Into my darkness, Maranatha.
Come, Lord Jesus.
Into my weakness, Maranatha.
Come, Lord Jesus.
Into my loneliness, Maranatha.
Come, Lord Jesus.
Into my fearfulness, Maranatha.
Come, Lord Jesus.
Come with your light.
Come in your power.
Come with your presence.
Come and encourage me, Maranatha.
Come, Lord Jesus.

I rejoice, for Christ comes: he is a light in my darkness.
He comes as of old, to those on the edge of a new day,
to those fearful and wanting to turn back,
to those with hard decisions to make,
to those who have been long in the desert. He comes.
I rejoice, for Christ comes: he is a light in my darkness.

He comes to all who are being challenged,
to those who are being overwhelmed,
to those who are facing a fiery ordeal,
to those longing for freedom,
to all who are seeking a better world. He comes.
I rejoice, for Christ comes: he is a light in my darkness.

He comes to those who live in simplicity,
to those who thirst for justice,
to those who hunger for righteousness,
to those who repent of their sins,
to those who turn away from evil. He comes.
I rejoice, for Christ comes: he is a light in my darkness.

He comes to those who seek to do his will,
who wait upon his word;
to all who magnify his name,
to all who rejoice in him as Saviour,
to each of us in our homes. He comes.
I rejoice, for Christ comes: he is a light in my darkness.

He comes to ordinary working people,
to all who are awake and alert,
to those going about their daily work,
to those who care for his creation,
to the humble and the meek. He comes.
I rejoice, for Christ comes: he is a light in my darkness.

He comes to the seekers and the searchers,
to all who will not be put off,
to those who travel in darkness,
to those not sure of their journey,
to everyone who offers their heart to him. He comes.
I rejoice, for Christ comes: he is a light in my darkness.

⊕

God, be my joy and strength;
God, be my light and guide;
God, be my hope and peace;
God, be with me this night and for ever.

COMMITTING ALL TO THE
____ LOVE OF THE LORD ____

Be thou my vision, O Lord of my heart;
be all else but naught to me, save that thou art;
be thou my best thought in the day and the night,
both waking and sleeping, thy presence my light.

Irish, eighth century
Translated by Mary Byrne (1880-1931)
Versified by Eleanor Hull (1860-1935)